ENCHIRIDION PARAMILITIS

ENCHIRIDION PARAMILITIS

THE POLICE HANDBOOK

MIKE OSUNA

ENCHIRIDION PARAMILITIS
THE POLICE HANDBOOK

iUniverse books may be ordered through booksellers or by contacting:

iUniverse
1663 Liberty Drive
Bloomington, IN 47403
www.iuniverse.com
844-349-9409

ISBN: 978-1-6632-2405-7 (sc)
ISBN: 978-1-6632-2406-4 (e)

Library of Congress Control Number: 2021911117

Print information available on the last page.

iUniverse rev. date: 06/16/2021

In loving memory of our Mother
Sylvia Osuna 2/22/53 - 1/13/09

CONTENTS

4. The Vices

INTRODUCTION

You are probably wondering what the title of this book means or perhaps what this book is about. The title of the book is in Latin and it simply means "Handbook of the paramilitary" (i.e. police, law enforcement, public service, etc.). Therefore, this handbook is intended for readers across a broad spectrum of fields as such and any person interested in becoming a better self and professional in their chosen field.

I became a Police Officer for the city of San Diego at the young age of 23. It was something I aspired doing as I was an explorer for National City at 16 and was an honor student graduate held at the Navy Seal Base in 1992.

I had the right disposition, the right character, and the right intentions to succeed in the law enforcement field and anywhere else for that matter.

You might be new to this career choice or perhaps you're a seasoned veteran (5 plus years). Throughout this book I will share my background, experiences, and discoveries about myself, and a thing called "the will" of man.

My purpose or "logos", is to create a dialogue about moral philosophy, ethics, and making right choices (i.e. the right time, the right way, for the right purpose). Now that you have become a professional is not the "telos" or result but a process that must be nurtured on a continual basis. This concept may be foreign but in practice it is an essential part of continual improvement training throughout industry.

I cannot tell you how important this dialogue is needed in a world so prevalent to corruption, moral degradation, and decline in virtue and teachings on the subject.

I hope you may find some tools in this shed that you can use today or sharpen the ones you have already and may have become dull in your life. This may be an opportunity of a lifetime because a lifetime is defined by your actions and the actions in the opportunity taken. My hope is that one may become self-aware of personal habits and self-assess the course they are currently taking. By doing so, changes can be made to chart a better result of what is defined as "self" and "Professional you"

I hope you will enjoy this book as you will learn a bit of Hebrew, Latin, and Greek. During a critical time in my past, I discovered a whole new world which opened my mind profoundly. The world which I knew had an origin of which I subconsciously chose to ignore until I asked, "from whence does it come?". In other words, I sought to understand the origin of word meanings and gathered historical data to better understand concepts, which turned beneficial in self-improvement.

MY FIRST ENCOUNTER – (PRIMO CONGRESSU)

It was a normal day in National City Ca. in 1985. My brother Rey and I decided to take my sister's banana seat bike to the local 7-11 store on Highland Ave. We lived on Second St., near National City Blvd. and now known as the Mile of Cars Way. My sister Veronica was a few years younger so she didn't mind us borrowing her bike. After all, she might have thought it was cute as it was a pink colored Huffy bike and to see both her older brother's cruising it would be priceless. Nonetheless, we were kids and going to 7-11 usually meant we would bring her back something sweet.

Those were good old days, I fondly remember, but something was to happen that totally would change the course of events in my life and make me the man who I am today! As we made it to 7-11, I stayed outside with my sister's bike and my brother made it in to pick up all the candy, soda, and ice cream we were supposed to take back home.

I was so excited, I decided to take my behind off the banana seat to look into the store and see if Rey didn't forget my whatchamacallit! As I stood there, two kids decided to jump on my sister's bike and take off with it. I started running after them as Rey came running out as well, perhaps he saw it all going down through the glass doors!

We tried catching up to those youngsters but all they did was laugh at our face as we stood there in the parking lot defenseless. I think I started to tear up as Rey, big brother that he was, rightly told me it was my fault for not watching our sister's bike.

We walked all the way home fighting about what happened and what we should've done to avoid getting our sister's bike stolen. Those were tough days and having a bike, no matter if it was a pink Huffy with a banana seat, two wheels were better than two heals!

We got home to break the news, not only to our baby sister, but Rey had to explain, being the eldest, how we managed to make it an unsuccessful trip to the store and had the bike stolen. It was hard enough raising three kids on her own, but our mother Sylvia, was always the nurturer and disciplinarian.

She knew exactly what to do and was able to make a phone call to summon the local policeman who got to our apartment within seconds. I've seen him around the neighborhood a few times but couldn't remember his name or what was going to happen. He asked us what happened and if we knew where the youngsters were last seen. He had us jump into his patrol cruiser as we sped to the 7-11.

Right around the corner from the 7-11 was those kids driving our sister's bike having the time of their' life. I mean literally, they were taking turns riding it and the look on their' faces once they saw us come out of the police car were like dears looking into headlights.

The police officer talked to the kids, gave us our bike back, and gathered some information from their' parents.

I felt so safe and protected around that officer that it must have given me a very deep and positive impression, as young as I was. He became my hero that very day and I remember thinking to myself perhaps someday I could grow up and help people feel the same way I felt that day. I don't remember his name but I did see him one last time.

I used to love seeing our mother cook as I would help her cut carrots and wash poultry for her. Years later, everyone always would complement our mother's cooking and how she made the best Mexican dishes. There was another thing our mother was well-known for and that was that she had a heart of gold for us kids. I mean, she always put our interest first and there were times she wouldn't eat so that we would have plenty to eat.

Years later, I saw pictures of her as a teen having very long beautiful hair, very thinly shaped and always with that same loving smile. I missed not having a father growing up and I remember I would tell our mother, "When I grow up I'm going to take my kids to buy them potato chips and sodas whenever they want!"

One day, I also recall waking up in the middle of the night as I often had trouble sleeping and made my way to the kitchen. I remember seeing our mom sitting on the couch next to a man I didn't know. I got to admit I was a bit frightened as it was lightly dimmed and didn't know what was going on.

I called out to our mother whom I ran to and held onto her very firmly and I didn't want to let go. She began to caress me and assured me everything was okay as she told me I should go back to bed. At that point, I looked over to the man that she was sitting with and I realized that it was the very police officer that had helped us get our sister's bike back.

I didn't know what to think but I did feel a bit awkward. I believe we all did and I remember he tried talking to me and asking me if I was okay. I was a very shy kid to begin with and didn't say a word but all I could do was not let go of our mother. A few minutes went by when finally I heard them whisper something to each other and the officer made his exit very quietly out the front door.

I never saw him again not even around the neighborhood but I did entertain the thought that I wish he could've been like my step-dad or something. Our mother and I never mentioned the event and/or I don't ever recall talking to my siblings about it. It was almost like a dream that subconsciously always remained in my psyche.

This very thing shaped the way I saw police officers and from that point on I knew that they were normal everyday people just like everybody else. The uniform stood in between my perception of them as regular citizens and American heroes, even while they were off-duty. This phenomenon persists into the fabric of society today and I believe will continue as long as there is public order, law, and administration of justice. It is of no surprise that for the early years of any American precinct or station their policy consisted of their' officers wearing uniforms off-duty. This brings me to the final point that wearing a badge and remaining a public official is a life-style and must not to be simply delegated as an occupation alone.

THE ACADEMY (HECADEMOS)

The founder of the first Academy in history took place in the 4th Century B.C. by the great philosopher Plato just North of Athens, Greece. It is legend that the name Hecademos was a hero who saved Athens from invasion 200 years prior. Plato was a student of the great philosopher Socrates and wrote many books including "The Republic". Our western civilization is built on some principles these men developed most notable the Dialectical form of reasoning. It is interesting that these great men both suffered misfortune at the hands of Justice in their' time. Socrates was sentenced to death and Plato at some point was sold into slavery but eventually died a free man. Yet, the Academy Plato founded was perhaps one of the earliest institutions of higher learning in history.

Under the Academy, an interesting slogan was said to be quoted "ἀγεωμέτρητος μὴ εἰσίτω. transliterated *ageometretos me eisito*, which is interpreted as "Those ignorant of geometry need not enter. Now breaking down this word we can find its true meaning. A- has the negative effect of any word such as a- in atheist (also a Greek word) thus, One who does *not* believe in God (Theo in Greek). Geo, of course means earth or the world. Now, metretos, has a very interesting meaning and it is found in the Greek writings of the other great philosopher Aristotle. It denotes the concept of measurement and the mean between excess and deficiency. This is a concept we will explore learning throughout this book as I learned through my experience in life, virtue and vice. "Me" means not and eisito to enter.

By reconstructing the phrase we can allow for a better understanding of this slogan. "Those who enter this academy must enter with the knowledge of the art of measurement."

One final note about this slogan is that our understanding about geometry now was very different 2400 years ago to the great originators of mathematics. Simply put, it's not about adding or subtracting your checkbook but about a way of life and the tool to be used in decision-making, awareness, and practical application in everyday situations. Thus, one becomes a philosopher. "Philios" meaning love and "Sophia" meaning wisdom and understanding.

Today, compulsory education teaches statistics, calculus etc. stuff we probably won't ever use again after high school or college. Well, Plato's academy wasn't in the business of manufacturing would- be tech geeks but would-be politician Greeks. This seems almost counterintuitive unless one has the grasp understanding that the "geometry" the academy had in mind was one that promotes the "good living in life". Those responsible for implementing the laws and enforcing the common good (i.e. politicians, lawyers, and statesmen) The whole idea of police officers is somewhat rather new in the whole scheme of history and are more properly addressed as paramilitary in this context.

So taking this into account, I can personally share my experience going through three police academies in my life, that today's Law enforcement academy is nothing like Plato's original academy. As any cop would tell you "Everything you learn in the academy...forget about it! Police work is learned on the job."

When I first started the academy it was class after class, quiz after quiz. Tactics. Introductions to the 3 branches of government and a very politically motivated video on ethics and sexual harassment. That's all for most part on lifestyle and becoming a successful cop. In fact, I often wondered how some of my peers became cops. There were open affairs between trainees and good old boy cliques between racial divides.

Granted it is no easy job and there are many distractions on the front line; money, women, drugs, etc. Being married and recently welcoming our firstborn Natalie, these issues were rarely talked about and much less the occupational factors like suicide, alcoholism, and divorce. I later learned that these three group factors make up a very high percentage among police officers. My intent is that the reader will grab a hold of the tools available and become aware in his or her decision-making as a professional.

TAKING THE OATH (IURANDUM)

The word itself pronounced "yourandoom" has the implication that one binds the law. As a Matter of fact, the root word "Iuris" means law and as Latin basics dictates, the letter I is pronounced as Y as there is no Y in the Latin alphabet.

When I was in Basic Academy I was an unsworn recruit applying myself: Mind, body, and Soul to the fundamentals of becoming a Police Officer. Even though I had many hours of discipline and studies, I did not become a full-fledged Official until I took the solemn oath. It was until I raised my right hand and declared before my Chief and Peers the principles and laws I would bind myself to uphold and live by that I was given the privilege to wear my badge #5674

I.......................DO SWEAR, THAT - I WILL WELL AND TRULY SERVE - OUR SOVEREIGN COUNTRY AND STATE - AS A POLICE OFFICER WITHOUT FAVOR OR AFFECTION - MALICE OR ILL-WILL - UNTIL I AM LEGALLY DISCHARGED, THAT I WILL SEE AND CAUSE OUR COMMUNITY'S PEACE TO BE KEPT AND PRESERVED - AND THAT - I WILL PREVENT TO THE

BEST OF MY POWER - ALL OFFENSES AGAINST THAT PEACE - AND THAT - WHILE I CONTINUE TO BE A POLICE OFFICER - I WILL - TO THE BEST OF MY SKILL AND KNOWLEDGE - DISCHARGE ALL THE DUTIES THEREOF - FAITHFULLY - ACCORDING TO LAW. SO HELP ME GOD.

I took this oath knowingly and willfully and repeated it as it was professed to me by my Superiors. This became my profession of faith and the scope of my calling that laid the code for my conduct on and off duty. Prior to this, I had studied the history of my agency and was surprised to find that patrolmen were to wear their uniforms at all times to serve as a reminder of this very oath. This therefore, is a testament that goes beyond a simple contract, beyond self, and goes to the furthest extant of the will to bestow.

There are many professions that take upon themselves this creed to bestow such as in the medical profession. The Hippocratic Oath is also a testament of the selfless confession physicians take to care for the weak and vulnerable. Ἱπποκράτης who lived in ancient Greece 5th Century BC is known as the father of western medicine. He standardized ethical principles by ritually having all new physicians swear by oath the will to uphold it to the upmost. This very oath is still used today in many medical schools around the world. Prior to World War II there had been a disuse of this oath as it was in Nazi Germany and the world witnessed the tragic outcome when decline in ethical standards occur in vital professions. As a matter of fact, at the famous Nuremberg trials, the doctors responsible for the extermination of millions of victims were tried and judged by this very oath.

In the very spectrum of paramilitary and militant professions the great statesman Cicero who lived in the 1st Century BC would have taken such an oath as he was also an investigator, Lawyer, and philosopher. Roman soldiers would strike at their' breastplates during inspections and shout "Integritas" which would create a sound ringing from the heart. This served to remind them of their' oaths and high moral standards and dedication to wholeness and of sound character. As the word itself, is a mathematical concept "Integer" meaning complete and undivided, a reference to the art of measurement of Plato's academy.

PROFESSIONAL LIFE (PROFESIONALIS VITAE)

In practically all Policy and procedure manuals there are descriptions of ethical standards, conduct, and how one must comport to hold a professional demeanor. In the agency I worked for, there was also a catch-all violation called conduct unbecoming of a police officer. I had a few co-workers whom after a lengthy investigation for alleged misconduct, sustained a demerit of conduct unbecoming. I didn't fully understand the implication of it all when I first heard of it and much less for a misconduct which happened off-duty. Perhaps, it meant all police officers were held to a higher standard and seemed like a double standard at times.

I began to think of the many job applications I submitted and the qualifications required of a police officer such as; must have a strong moral character and be in good standing in the community. I believe these qualifications are what agencies struggled with the most in finding in any recruit. In California, there are many college campuses, coffee houses, and book stores filled with degree-holding and unemployed prospects. Agencies seek out not only the moldable and courageous but also the most noble and benevolent of citizens.

Philosophers of old always held virtue to be the key in "being and becoming" in a sense of sustainment and substance. I remember a recruit I attended the academy with, after passing probation, kicked up his feet on the table and said, "I don't have to do shit now that I'm off probation!" I thought it funny at the time because of all the hard work, stress, and discipline our training demanded. I often wondered if that same recruit was still wearing a uniform. What I do realize now is that perhaps at one point in my 7 year career I said those very words inside myself and stopped becoming that peace officer I once was when I first started.

It is true that we are our own worst enemy and a change happens inside each of us that must be checked. Perhaps, the root cause is power but the end result could be good or could be bad and it is left for us to choose. As President Abraham Lincoln once said to test the true character of a man, give him power. This is what happened when I became a police officer. I was given a gun and a badge for the purpose of upholding the oath I swore and professionalism was the art of keeping it.

I believe professionals are made, not born. Whether they are police officers, soldiers or lawyers. This is a matter of choice that can be acquired by disposition and practice. However, there are those born with a natural disposition by virtue and by virtue, behavioral. Just like a carpenter is a carpenter because he builds and a teacher because she teaches. The question is do they do it well and if so how. This is my intent and by bringing awareness, foster intelligence into becoming and upholding a professional life.

HABITS (MORIBUS)

The word habit or habeo simply means "to have" in Latin and it is actually the vestment a nun wears over her head. It can also mean to live as in a habitat. However put, demonstrates a necessity, whether it is something acquired or given by nature.

Before I became a Police Officer, I had many habits, both good and bad. I had a natural inclination towards good habits such as being respectful, honest, and self-motivated. I also had a natural inclination towards bad habits such as being impatient, desiring too much of something or the wrong thing at the wrong time. Over time, I purged myself of bad habits and acquired new habits. This is a task that I learned through training, experience, and right thought.

The objective is a choice which asserts the statement "I am a good person! Therefore, I will make right and good choices" Choose good habits and I will have good character or choose bad habits and I will have bad character. Although a good person may have a few bad habits he makes them smaller or makes them less than the good ones so that they are more discreet and not as serious. Although a bad person may have a few good habits he makes no effort of making them bigger or more than the bad ones and continues to make the bad ones more noticeable and more serious. This makes up a mean or an average of which one will become defined as. Many Greek philosophers defined this as the balance between excess and deficiency. For example, Courage is the mean between fearfulness and rashness and liberality is the mean between stinginess and wastefulness.

The purpose of the police academy was to expose me to a new mean and to build muscle memory into my psyche. I developed simple habits such as always having my strong hand free and never leaving my hands in my pockets. These are simply rules but others I acquired during training so that I would do them automatically without thought and with ease. So that when under stress and danger I would be steadfast in my spirit without immobilizing fear.

Those that acquired this new mean would graduate and receive a P.O.S.T certificate or Peace Officer's Standard and Training Certificate. Those that did not make it were those that missed the mark and were unable to properly aim for the target. So it became important to know just where I stood in terms of that mean in order to aim correctly and hit the mark.

Through my life experience and training it became evident that this was just as true in my professional life as it was in my personal life but not without struggle.

IDENTITY CONFLICT (CONFLICTUS IDENTITATEM)

Throughout my years of service, I became accustomed to behaving myself less like a cop once I took off my uniform and therefore I developed a sense of an Identity crisis. This was due to my expected aim in life and my role in society clashing together. Identity is a very strong phenomenon that rips to the core question of "Who am I?" and "What's my purpose?". In my role as a cop; I was selfless, Law abiding, virtuous, and Heroic. For my service I expected gratitude, respect, honor, and praise all the time everywhere. Reality was not the case and this was a formula of self-destruction as I began to drink heavily and pursued extramarital affairs. Once this formula of Hubris set in, it was like quicksand bringing confusion and tragedy after tragedy.

The only way out was to face reality, accept my fate, and accept my identity. I chose the identity of police officer as a profession, the identity of father by begetting, the identity of drunkard by binge drinking, and the identity of ex-police officer by exiting the profession. The difference between what I chose to identify with and what others identified me with is a matter of discussion as many are quick to judge others. "Who I am" can take many aspects of self and the way I saw myself and the way I saw others. Therefore, once I became a police officer I decided to associate myself from "undesirables" and more with other like-minded police officers. I began to see others as "bad" by legal definition of my own making. I said within myself that I must be one of the noblest persons there is just because I stood for the common good and served and protected the innocent. I began to question the motives of others and held many in suspicion because they were not in law enforcement.

Perception and Identity are like two brothers, one black and one white, they identify their' identical nature to the same parents and family. However, perception has it that just because he is black he is treated better or worse than his brother and vice versa. The question of "What I am" is something attributed to the nature of a person and "Who I am" is an attribute of the person and what character that person takes. For example, I will always be human, and it defines "What I am". A human is not perfect and is capable of mistakes as the famous phrase goes "Errare Humanum est." or "to err is human". This word Errare is a Latin term that means to wander or stray from the straight path. It can become very difficult to differentiate what someone is and who they really are, thus an identity conflict.

MY WEAKNESSES
(INFIRMITATEM MEAM)

Perhaps there is a point in time in everyone's life when they must ask themselves "Do I really know myself?" That point in time came to me when I was given the opportunity to serve my country as a police officer. I was vested with such great powers to arrest, to carry a firearm, and to enforce the laws meant to keep society safe from evildoers. I believe I was given this responsibility because I carried myself with integrity, courage, and discipline. I strived to be as honest as I could to the point where if I found a $5 dollar bill on the ground I would try to find its rightful owner. My courageousness measured to the caliber of stopping a thief from robbing a convenient store and my discipline resembled that of a Navy Seal in combat. Indeed, my self-assessment was based on standards that were ideal and romanticized by heroism.

As I became exposed to real life situations and crisis events, I was expected to solve societies ills and I would become the savior personification of the law. That standard that I once held shifted slightly off balance to what I was accustomed to and the numbness became a coping mechanism to shield off emotional attachments. My weakness, then came to me like a lightning rod separating what I thought I knew and what I knew about myself. I had trained in three academies, earned a college degree, and even taught bible studies but I hadn't learned the most important subject of self. Knowing history, math, or science could teach me things about myself but could not equate knowing who I was. A Roman African philosopher in the 5th century A.D known as St. Augustine discovered this great truth about knowledge, knowledge of self, and love of self. "Mens, Notitia Sui, Amor Sui".

I had obtained discipline, integrity, and courage through knowledge but knowledge of self was needed to maintain moderation and the art of measurement. Love of self was the final step that embodied all the virtues that I would later learn through life's struggles and set-backs. As Aristotle once said that virtue has no teachers but moral virtue can be learned by forming habits. I had obtained knowledge about how to keep out of trouble growing up in my neighborhood, about making something of myself through education, and about religious experience that made me see the world in a different perspective.

I had reached the first step into this triad of self-understanding by obtaining knowledge of the virtues but I didn't know where I stood on the continuum as I had not gaged myself upon such spectrum. In order to gage myself, I had not sought to know myself, but by accidents of excess and deficiency I had come to know who I really was. To this end, not knowing myself was my greatest weakness and I accepted the misconception that whatever I exceeded in must be virtuous and whatever I lacked in was not virtuous.

MY STRENGTHS (VIRIUM MEARUM)

"Scientia potentia est" was a phrase coined by Sir Francis Bacon in 1597 and is translated as "Knowledge is power". Sir Francis Bacon was also famous for developing the inductive reasoning that is used today in the scientific method of conducting research in many fields of science. After achieving many titles in London England such as Attorney General and Lord Chancellor, he was later impeached for corruption and bribery. Despite Sir Francis' weaknesses, his major accomplishments and contributions to science is what is remembered most of his character. Such is the case with many political figures today and many successful and noble people who have succumbed to the notion of invincibility. I believe it would be safe to say that such exceptional people knew where their' strengths lie in comparison to their weaknesses as if the balance on a scale would tip to the side of strength. In other words, I would agree that knowing where excess lies would be easier than knowing where deficiency lies. Take, for example, honesty. It would be easy to say that if many great and successful leaders would be more honest with themselves or others than there would be less corruption in the world.

Taking a closer look into this matter would also beg the question of just how much more honest? So, then the question or answer would deduct to "more than" or "less than" in terms of having such a thing as honesty. As a police officer I was expected to be honest with my partners, superiors, and the public. However, when it came to criminals or suspects It was almost a thing of weakness to show honesty as a means of communication and even a necessary evil to use deceitfulness for advantage. Some may have called it the "gift of gab" or others "creative speaking" but whatever terms were used, the means seemed justified by the ends. To a criminal mind, being smarter than the average person, means having more advantage than the next person in order to gain something in return. To a cop, this meant shifting standards in order to achieve that advantage. So much that a good cop would be considered a "good cop" by being able to choose the lesser of two evils in regards to quick decision making and discretion.

PARADIGM SHIFT (TANGIBILEM)

The balance then lies between excess and deficiency as the scales of justice typically exemplify. A calibration must be made as to the standard unit of measurement as in weights and measures on a table. For example, there are customary units for liquids, length, and energy whereby they must be measured for accuracy and standardization. The first emperor of Rome Augustus Caesar introduced lady iustitia (yoosteetsia) which goes back to ancient Greek and Egyptian mythology. The ancient world viewed mostly everything having balance must be a result of weight and measures. Even such intangible things such as Prudence, justice, fortitude, and temperance. The very things that are material facts found in the halls of justice. Originally, lady justice was not blind folded to impartiality in regards to power, wealth, or prestige when rendering justice. Perhaps, due to the reality of practical application that is typical throughout history. The scale lacked a foundation as to allow for the evidence to stand for itself as in the preponderance of the evidence, probable cause, or beyond a reasonable doubt test.

By definition, a weight is how much force gravity acts on a given amount of mass something has. As science dictates, force of gravity differs depending on what part of the earth is measured, much more planets. As humans, we are microcosmos, worlds within communities whereby balance, harmony, justice and injustice take place. As a cop, I became exposed to the injustices of modern life and witnessed the worst side of humanity. Cynicism ran its course, and I developed a false perspective of life and individuals. This affected the way I carried myself and the attitude I adopted in my professional discourse and personal lifestyle. By natural law, I was headed on a broad path down-stream until something, someone, or myself caused a realignment.

I began to rethink values and morality and the possibility that such things as virtue and vice could actually gage me on a whole new level. I thought, perhaps the law was not my ultimate teacher in morals and conduct of living but a border of where boundaries lie. This is evident as history has shown that to live in a draconian society will not create the best human possible but rather a prison state, whether mental or physical. Draco (Δράκων) was Athens Greece first law-giver in the 7th century B.C. and he is said to have created the harshest penalties for the most minor offenses. The more lenient of penalties went to the most privileged members of society but even Draconian Greece has not created more laws than today's American justice system. So, if not by law than by what means can one reach moral excellence? Has not the law defined who a morally excellent person is (i.e. police officer, an attorney, judge, etc.).

The Greek definition of moral excellence is arete (ἀρετή) which means to live up to one's full potential and make use of all one's faculties or moral virtue. In the Roman world, arete translated into virtue and by definition comes from the word vir which simply means man. In other words a human (man or woman) will reach moral excellence when they reach something higher than bestial instincts, attain contemplation, and conquer their passions. So, what comes of being an excellent man or woman? Praise? honor? Self-respect? What about power, wealth and prestige? Does full power corrupt? Does extreme wealth bring happiness? Or does prestige depend only on perception? All these in of themselves are not bad but in excess become troublesome just like virtue which is defined as the golden mean between excess and deficiency.

In order to understand all of one's faculties that make up virtue we must look at individual virtues and contemplate what makes them virtue, what constitutes its excess and where does deficiency lie. Once identified, the targeted goal must be practiced and repeated over and over so that it will become "2nd nature" and an excellent product will be achieved. For example, many successful businesses have adopted a quality strategy best remembered by an acronym DMAIC. Define, Measure, Analyze, Improve, and Control. If successful businesses use this model to improve and better their products than why can't a person use this model to improve their quality of life? Perhaps, this is what the great philosopher Aristotle provided us with a working model on how to improve oneself, ones life, and bring out the best of persons. The police academies, law schools, boot camps are a factory of persons that serve the public good and professionals are their products. Just like today companies design, plan, and produce new technologies so did the ancient world in producing the true politic or statesman.

PRUDENCE (PRUDENTIAE)

Prudence is defined as the ability to discern the appropriate course of action to be taken in a given situation at the appropriate time. Although it is not an action it is used to foresee the cause and effect of one's actions and regulate all other virtues. For example, if a cat straddles the fence it is inevitable that the cat will choose one side of the fence. It is only a matter of time the cat will react, whether moved by fear or instinct as animals are said to not have the ability to choose by reason of good or bad. For the sake of discussion, let's just say good means the lesser of two evils or the middle road and not the extremes. The bad we will call the excess or the deficiency which are either of the two extremes.

In terms of taking the appropriate course of action let's say you observe a pedestrian walking down the street and in your normal patrol duties you stop him to investigate. Does prudence dictate a lawful stop where you have reasonable suspicion, or do you just want to talk to the pedestrian because of personal bias? Prudence deals with knowledge which governs actions so knowledge will increase discernment on the appropriate course to take and at what time. So the pedestrian taking one step into traffic might just be the proper time for engagement and intervening for their safety.

Prudence is also said to be an intellectual virtue versus an ethical virtue such as the following ones we will be discussing. There are many case laws which hinge upon reasoning and sway to one conclusion rather than the other and this is due to prudence. It is the starting point in which actions are executed and the means to the ends accomplished. We must always ask the question why I did such thing or why did I not act in a certain way. To delve much deeper into the matter, the most prudent choice will be the one that was thought about most thoroughly as would make most practical sense.

JUSTICE (IUSTITIAE)

Justice is said to be a cardinal virtue as it hinges upon every virtue as much as the hinges on a door allows entry or exit. Many interested in law will at some point study administration of justice or criminal justice but what does it really mean? It might sound like a complicated term but it is really something we all practice everyday from the time we grow up and reach adolescence we come to understand what our roles are inside the family unit, at school, at work and amongst friends. It is a balance of giving your fair share and taking what is rightfully and legally yours. So, in other words it is based on fairness and law. However, not all things that are legal are fair even though we all might want what is our equal share. For example, society grants minors emancipation at 18 years of age but they cannot enjoy certain rights until they reach the age of 21.

So, if justice is the mean then what are the extremes? Justice is the moderation between Selfishness and selflessness and it is used to regulate relationships with others. In terms of criminal justice, if a citizen commits robbery using force or fear against another citizen the law administers a deemed felony and imprisonment, regardless of the value of what was robbed. So then if this citizen is now a felon because of actions taken then why did this person commit this act in the first place? Could it be that selfishness dictated that the object robbed was held in such value that no matter how hard that person worked to attain, it could never be achievable?

Take into consideration that of the victim who has worked very hard to attain such object robbed from their' person. Maybe in a different case it was known to the criminal that the object was given to the victim and perceives that no true loss will be suffered. Either way, if the criminal would have given measure to thought and weighed in on the virtue of justice, between selfishness and selflessness. Perhaps, a more formidable opinion on the matter could be ascertained such as the value of freedom far outweighing the value of the desired object. If selflessness is considered, then the thought of suppression of desire may be a reasonable cause to abort such irrational behavior.

In any case, if the accused stands trial with a reasonable defense or faces a prisoner's dilemma to choose the lesser of two evils, where then does justice lie? How about for the victim? For Police, this is just a matter for the court to decide and if there is probable cause that a crime was committed and that the suspect in question most likely committed the crime then this is justice. So, justice may be different to different persons and to certain circumstances depending on what is considered a selfish act and what is a selfless one. This may be an issue based on equity of which civil law is concerned and makes up for the offset between what is fair and what is legal.

In personal relationships there is such a thing as the law of reciprocity whereby what is given an equal share is expected in return. This reciprocity law at times does not apply such as when a gift is given from a father to a son. This

Mike Osuna

is also by deductive reasoning based on discretion, which is free will and exercise of justice, something of which police officers have a great deal of while working on patrol.

One final note on justice translated in Hebrew is צדק (Tzedek) which is about righting wrongs. As in every society, there are governments which make the underrepresented vulnerable to oppression and abuse. By looking deeper into its root word Tzedek is not only about deciding cases in a court of law but also about substantive views which share the meaning with the Hebrew word for charity Tzedakah. When given thought between these two seemingly different words feeling is at the core of charitable action versus judicial action which is said to be free from all bias, feelings, and preferential treatment. Clearly measure should be taken into account so that things are not simply as they are but as they ought to be.

FORTITUDE (FORTITUDINE)

Fortitude is translated from the Greek word for courage ἀνδρεία and is also one of four cardinal virtues which is the mean between fear and confidence or cowardness and rashness. It is said to be the most essential of all virtues as it is the thing used to hold all other virtues together in times of crisis. Courage is the will that drives virtues into fruition, but prudence and justice give measure and balance. Without this balance courage shifts to the extremes and become vices. This virtue is chief amongst badge and honor for it represents valor and bravery in the face of danger.

The term reasonable force comes into play whenever criminal apprehension is at issue before, during, or after apprehension. Reasonable force is something which holds courage at the center of discussion as it can mean many different things dependent on the circumstances. It can also differentiate an officer's conduct between a cowardly act or an act of bravery. Too many times has an officer's actions seem cowardly by the simple fact that he or she yielding power reacts with obvious fear to subdue and overcome. Justice or injustice become evident with a slight display of courage or its vices become manifest for an action committed in fear. Vices as we have said are excess or deficiencies of the targeted goal or simply put evils, and virtues are the goods of action.

In Hebrew thought, virtue and vice are translated יֵצֶר הָרַע (Yetzer Hara) and means inclination to do evil and יֵצֶרהטּוֹב (Yetzer HaTov) means the inclination to do good. The inclination to do evil is said that we are inherently born with and it is the misuse of things we need for survival. For example, the need to eat and drink at its excess becomes drunkenness and gluttony. Every basic hierarchy of need has its own set of excesses and deficiencies and therefore children are more prone to seek excesses because they have not learned balance between inclination to do evil and inclination to do good and lack experience.

This can be found in western Judeo-Christian origins which has rendered different translations throughout history and into law such as the division between criminal law and juvenile law which seeks mostly rehabilitation versus punishment. This is due to the belief that the will to choose between right and wrong and according to law abidance is stronger as one becomes an adult and reaches maturity.

The issue of free will has been debated for centuries but the fact remains that there is always a choice. Courage is the catalyst to this choice and to aim for the mean and avoid excesses in virtues and deficiencies by choosing moderation in terms of meeting the hierarchy of needs.

TEMPERANCE (TEMPERANTIA)

Temperance is defined as the mean or moderation of thought, action and feeling and in its primitive form showing restraint when it comes to eating and drinking. In other words, it is exercising self-restraint and self-control by forming a habit of moderation in regard to indulgence and appetite. This also includes having restraint from the impulse of using force or anger.

Temperance comes from the Greek word εγκράτεια (egkratea) and is translated as having strength of will or character. I remember during a police interview I was asked a simply question "What would you do if you saw your partner stealing a candy bar?" This question may have seemed like a trick question at the time, but it delves deep into the issue of temperance. Any acceptable answer could have ranged between telling on your partner or offering your partner to pay for the snack.

Having Temperance is the mean between overindulgence ακολασία (akolasia) and being numb as Insensible αναισθησία (anaisthesia) as to pleasure and pain. There is a correlation between the passions and emotions and the way one consumes food and particularly alcoholic beverage. This is a tenet that many ex-alcoholics have learned in order to become sober and get a handle on their dependency to alcohol. Alcoholism to many ex-alcoholics is said to be a symptom of underlying emotions such as fear, anger, depression, and guilt.

As I began my career in law enforcement I rarely drank alcohol but as years flew by I found myself overindulging in alcohol without even realizing what I was going through or what the future lay ahead. The more I drank the more I believed I could tolerate getting drunk and led myself to make wrong choices of which I later realized hurt loved ones closest to me and myself.

In a state of over-indulgence, my aim for the mark became blurred and prudence and justice for me became satisfying my appetite of which was never to be filled completely. Enjoyment of life and the good of life I learned must be taken with measure for without good measure it is not good.

In order to become an excellent officer of the law one must practice self-discipline on a daily basis, on and off duty. The Greek word for self-discipline σωφρονισμοῦ (sophronismo) can also be translated as self-restraint, sound judgement and self-control. One must start with inner self to form a character that is worthy of displaying the badge which represents honor.

UNREASONABLENESS (IRRATIONABILITAS)

In order to begin discussion regarding the vices we will look at the virtue of prudence of which is the mean between imprudence and false prudence. Vice as we have said is either a deficiency or the excess of that virtue. In other words, not enough prudence will result in no prudence to begin with and too much of prudence may lead to false prudence (or false reasoning)

We have defined Prudence as the ability to discern the appropriate course of action to be taken in a given situation at the appropriate time. So imprudence may be defined as not having the ability to discern the appropriate course of action in a given situation and at the wrong time. We can better understand the word unreasonableness as the vice which covers both the excess and the deficiency by its Greek translation παραλογισμός (Paralogismos).

Paralogism is actually an English word which means the same and is defined as having fallacious argument or illogical conclusion, especially one committed by mistake or believed by the person to be logical. So when an action is committed on the grounds of false prudence it is because they believe the right action was taken, therefore proves the inability of discernment. In its Latin definition this simply means irrational and illogical conclusions.

To combat lack of discernment in order to reach reasonableness and true prudence one must deliberate, seek counsel and commit to action as to the best course to take. It is best that once counsel is achieved that it is also understood and agreed to as the true and right course. This may take but a few minutes and up to a few days depending on the circumstance involved but it should not be confused with being overly cautious.

Vice is a common police Jargon word often associated with crimes involving illegal sales of alcohol, prostitution, narcotics, and gambling. Just like vice units seek out to curtail immoral activities so too should an officer seek out to reduce in extent personal vices and increase in quantity the amounts of virtue one can possess. This concept also applies to obtaining any virtuous thing by means of dishonest gains. In other words, the ends do not justify the means.

UNFAIRNESS (INIQUITATES)

Unfairness deals with what is unequal and unjust. Specifically, in terms of character and actions, it is something that is based on a person's unjust actions or being unjust. Now, there is a difference between the two but many treat these as though they are the same thing. For Example, when one offends or commits a felony they will be branded for life as a felon or an offender. It does not matter how many just acts this person may have done that will change the belief that one felony committed is one person's deemed character.

To this purpose Law enforcement is entrusted to equalize public disorder and to protect those who cannot protect themselves. Such as from those who would take advantage of the weak and laws are enacted to be just and equal. So, what is lawful is said to be just and fair. So when certain laws are found to be unjust or unfair the governed may have recourse by way of process and procedure dependent on government form.

I remember taking tactical and defense training in the academy whereby we were taught not to fight fair but to always gain the upper hand. For example, if a suspect raised a fist, we raised a baton. If a suspect brandished a weapon such as a knife, we would be justified in using lethal force. Then this approach was modified later to include less then nonlethal force. Whatever the case the outcome always mandated to overcome the threat by way of what was reasonable and necessary.

The fact of the matter is that life isn't fair and not everything or everyone is equal and laws exist to govern. As I grew in my career the more I realized this truth and witnessed firsthand how people learned to take advantage of laws, the legal system and became successful at it. I saw the unjust prosper and the just become oppressed by the very system that is meant to create balance and order. At some point I felt I was the only one to stand between that balance or imbalance and my discretion was to allow it to exist or set order to things.

COWARDICE (INCREPITA IGNAVIA)

Cowardice is the deficiency of courage and rashness the excess of courage. Simply put, courage is the action we want to project as a defined virtue and rashness is the excess that is to be avoided. However, rashness is closer to the mean of courage than cowardice is so in this regard should not rashness be sought more than cowardice?

By virtue of becoming a police officer it is evident that courage is a necessary character trait in respect to enforcing laws and apprehending criminals. There is also a natural inclination to one of either vice but when displaying a hint of cowardice, it is easy to leap into actions which appear more courageous than the next person. This phenomenon is embedded in such cultures where acts of bravery and courage are most honorable.

Cowardice has an underlying emotion of fear and is rectified by training, tactics and enforced by habitual drills during the academy. This creates the state of balanced action and sets the expectation of what is deemed proper for any situation that has been created as real-life scenarios.

OVERINDULGENCE (INDULGENTIA)

To indulge is not something which is inherently wrong or incorrect as it is normal to enjoy what one desires such as food, drink, work, speech, sex, or go shopping. An average person may enjoy all these things sometime but not all the time and not every time. There is a balance between pleasure and pain and if temperance is that balance then executing any of the items listed, in excess, is the vice.

The Latin translation of indulgence is indulgeo which means to permit or to allow. So, to overindulge would mean to allow self to gratify needs and wants to excess. This may not be about how many times an act is committed but may be more about what one is committing excessively. There are detrimental consequences to character when permit is granted over one simple act and or over time can build up.

As discussed, in regard to virtue there are usually two vices, a deficiency and an excess but in this case I would like to identify the deficiency would be lack of enjoyment. Temperance is the virtue that can constitute to what point enjoyment is fulfilled and if not achieved the end result will be pain. Someone devoid of food, drink, work etc. will experience pain until their experience can teach them the know-how to use temperance as the key to be living in balance.

Nature may dictate what one is more inclined to indulge in, but nurture may help regulate the choices which will ultimately form the character of self. There are those who have abstained from gratifying needs and wants in order to achieve a respectable position of power, such as a cop, an attorney, a judge and then opportunity and time presents revisitation to that need or want. This is why it is said that power is the true test of character.

Police departments always conduct background checks in order to verify temperance in terms of drug usage, alcohol and or other peculiar habits of an individual. In addition, a psychological exam and evaluation is accomplished in order to delve into the mind of the perspective candidate.

CONCLUSION

There are persons who identify themselves with their profession as a calling or perhaps because of hard work and perseverance, validation. There are those who set the standard of what they call real good police work by their daily conduct. Where you are in life and where you stand will be a determining factor on how your conduct will be acceptable or unacceptable, regardless of how many merits earned. The para-militant subculture is such that projects a black and white linear worldview.

Every person inducted into this hall of justice has their story of why they chose their given profession. Whether because they themselves were once victims or they have certain predatory traits that seemed like a perfect fit to cause hate and discontent. The fact of the matter is, public servants are just that, public servants of the people. Some notable figures have ranged from Cicero to Paul the apostle of which history has shown their good and bad deeds based on standards of their times.

I am one of those who have walked in the shoes of brass wearing uniformed personnel and have committed acts which has tarnished reputation and honor. Nonetheless, lessons learned deserves attention and heeded warning to all who fall in the spectrum of law enforcement. We are not just ex-cops or has-beens but a community such as POW's, veterans and citizens who have performed civic duties.

The Art of measurement is one of many tools available to you to have a very long and successful career and lifestyle. The key is finding that balance and accepting the fact that you are not invincible and or above the law. You are a servant above all and your actions determine the quality of your person.

	LESS THAN (-)	MEAN μ	MORE THAN (+)
DOMAINS	DEFICIENCY	VIRTUE	EXCESS
THOUGHT	IMPRUDENCE	PRUDENCE	FALSE PRUDENCE
ACTION	SELFLESSNESS	JUSTICE	SELFISHNESS
FEELING	COWARDICE	COURAGE	RASHNESS
ACTION	INSENSIBLE	TEMPERANCE	OVERINDULGENCE
SELF-ASSESSMENT			
	LESS THAN (-)	MEAN μ	MORE THAN (+)
DOMAINS	DEFICIENCY	VIRTUE	EXCESS

Table 1

Depicts how thoughts, actions and feelings develop into Self. Our Character is then formed by virtue (the mean between two extremes).

ENABLERS	LESS THAN (-)	MEAN μ	MORE THAN (+)
	DEFICIENCY	VIRTUE	EXCESS
PEOPLE			
PLACES			
THINGS			

Table 2

Identifies how enablers influence our targeted goal of virtue (the mean between two extremes)

BIBLIOGRAPHY

Aristoteles, Aristotle, K., T. J. A., & Tredennick, H. (2004). *The Nicomachean ethics*. Penguin.

Plaut, W. G., Bamberger, B. J., & Hallo, W. W. (1996). In *Torah = The Torah: a modern commentary*. introduction, Union of American Hebrew Congregations.

Marshall, A. (1987). In *NASB-NIV Parallel New Testament in Greek and English*. Regency.

Hursthouse, R., & Pettigrove, G. (2016, December 8). *Virtue Ethics*. Stanford Encyclopedia of Philosophy. https://plato.stanford.edu/entries/ethics-virtue/.

WirelessPhilosophy. (2015, September 8). *PHILOSOPHY - The Good Life: Aristotle [HD]*. YouTube. https://www.youtube.com/watch?v=VFPBf1AZOQg.

Hursthouse, R., & Pettigrove, G. (2016, December 8). *Virtue Ethics*. Stanford Encyclopedia of Philosophy. https://plato.stanford.edu/entries/ethics-virtue/.

gbisadler. (2013, November 29). *The Virtue of Courage in Aristotle's Nicomachean Ethics - Philosophy Core Concepts*. YouTube. https://www.youtube.com/watch?v=KSHqHQzIZ3g.

YouTube. (2020, July 13). *Temperance (Aquinas 101)*. YouTube. https://www.youtube.com/watch?v=9BU1zMipFcA.

Latin Dictionary Online Translation LEXILOGOS. (n.d.). https://www.lexilogos.com/english/latin_ dictionary.htm.

A Hippocratic Oath for policing. National Police Foundation. (2020, April 8). https://www.policefoundation. org/a-hippocratic-oath-for-policing/.

Baird, F. E., & Kaufmann, W. A. (2007). *Modern philosophy*. Prentice Hall.

Wikimedia Foundation. (2021, April 27). *Francis Bacon*. Wikipedia. https://en.wikipedia.org/wiki/Francis_ Bacon.

Wikimedia Foundation. (2021, May 4). *Cicero*. Wikipedia. https://en.wikipedia.org/wiki/Cicero.

Erasmus, D., & Erasmus, D. (1624). *Des. Erasmi Roterodami, Enchiridion militis christiani*. Apud A. Cloucquium.

GLOSSARY OF LATIN WORDS

Paramilitis - Paramilitary
Enchiridion - Handbook
Fabula - Story
Primo Congressu - First Encounter
Hecademos - Academy
Iurandum - Taking oath
Profesionalis Vitae - Professional Life
Moribus - Habits
Conflictus Identitatem - Identity Conflict
Infirmitatem - Weakness
Virium - Strength
Tangibilem - Paradigm Shift
Prudentiae - Prudence
Iustitiae - Justice
Fortitudine - Fortitude, Courage
Temperantia - Temperance
Irrationabilitas - Unreasonableness
Iniquitates - Unfairness
Increpita Ignavia - Cowardice
Indulgentia - Overindulgence

GLOSSARY OF GREEK WORDS (TRANSLITERATED)

Λόγος - Reason, Logic, Purpose

ἀγεωμέτρητος μὴ εἰσίτω (ageometretos me eisito) - Those ignorant of geometry need not enter.

ἀρετή (arete) - Moral Excellence

ἀνδρεία (andreia) - Courage

εγκράτεια (egkrateia) - Temperance, Self-Control

αναισθησία (anaisthesia) - Insensible, Indifference

ακολασία (akolasia) - Overindulgence, Lack of Restraint

σωφρονισμοῦ (sophronismou) - Soundness of thought, Self-Control

παραλογισμός (paralogismos) – Fallacy of Thought, Illogical Conclusion

GLOSSARY OF HEBREW WORDS (TRANSLITERATED)

צדק (tzedek) - Justice

יֵצֶר הָרַע (yetzer Hara) - Inclination to do bad.

יֵצֶרהטוֹב (yetzer Hatov) - Inclination to do good.

Printed in the United States
by Baker & Taylor Publisher Services